NATURALLY RAISE YOUR BABY

Use the Continuum Concept to Bring Up a Healthy and Well-Rounded Child

Table of Contents

Introduction

I want to thank you and congratulate you for downloading this book. By doing so, you are taking the first necessary step in becoming the parent that your child deserves. You will learn about some of the best techniques to raise a happy, healthy boy or girl. And, isn't that what all parents want for their child?

Being a parent today can be incredibly stressful. All around you, people are giving advice and articles are being published, all of them with conflicting ideas. This makes it nearly impossible to decide how to raise a child.

Have you ever heard that if you hold your baby too much or respond every time they cry, it will spoil them? This is an old wives' tale that has been disproven time and time again. Still, however, there are many women who hear this and believe it to be true.

The Continuum Concept is the opposite of the above method of raising a child. Under the Continuum Concept, you hold your baby more and respond to their needs. However, you do so in a way that does not make them feel as if they are the center of the world. In this way, they are not spoiled.

Have you ever studied how 'less-civilized' or older tribes of people would raise their children? Often, babies had a very close relationship with their parents. Their needs were always fulfilled and they developed close bonds with their parents, because they were often held constantly by their parents or other close family members. Babies were often breastfed on demand, rather than being forced to eat on a schedule.

The result of this closeness was happier babies and happier adults. This fact was learned when an explorer and author named Jean Liedloff spent two-and-a-half years with the Yequana tribe of South America. During this time, she studied the differences in their culture and the culture of Westerners. Not only did the tribe raise their children differently, Liedloff described the Yequana tribe as some of the happiest people she had ever met. One of the factors that she attributed this to during her five studies was the major differences in the way that the Yequana tribe raised their babies, especially when compared with some of the common Western child rearing practices.

This book, *Naturally Raise Your Baby: Use the Continuum Concept to Bring Up a Healthy and Well-Rounded Child*, will teach you the principles of the Continuum Concept. You will learn about how to go back to your ancestral roots and raise your babies with love and care, so that they become healthy, well-rounded, and happy adults.

Chapter One: An Overview of the Continuum Concept

The Continuum Concept is about using more traditional methods of child rearing, such as breastfeeding on demand, immediately responding to your baby's needs, co-sleeping, etc. The major reason to raise your child in this way is to stimulate healthy, happy development.

The Yequana Tribe of South America

Jean Liedloff is the greatest influencer of the Continuum Concept, being the woman who researched and wrote about the topic. Liedloff made five separate expeditions to the Venezuelan Rainforest of South Africa. In total, she would spend 2 ½ years with the tribe.

The thing that sets the Yequanas apart from many other tribes is their isolation from Western society. The Yequanas are often referred to as a 'stone age' tribe, because their isolation has encouraged them to keep their primitive practices. While these practices span beyond just child rearing, it was their child raising practices that interested Liedloff. As you read this book, you will learn more about the practices of the Yequana tribe and how the way they raise their children contributes to a happier, healthier existence.

What is Wrong with Current Child-Rearing Practices?

For those who live in Western culture, each century that passes brings parents farther and farther from their natural parental instincts. The problem is that as parents distance themselves from these instincts, the consequences of children's behavior become more prominent. Children and adolescents are paying the price for this. Some practices would never have been considered in earlier times. The result of these changes and this disconnect between parents and their children include:

1. Weakened parent-child relationships, especially for children who spend a lot of time away from their parents (such as when both parents work or the child frequently goes to a sitter or daycare)

2. Child and adolescent depression, often caused by a disconnect from parents and a difficult time adjusting to other adults or children

3. Unmet childhood needs, which can lead to poor social and mental development, and possibly problems like self-esteem

4. Problems like post-partum depression in mothers and issues like ADHD (attention deficit hyperactive disorder), SIDS (sudden infant death syndrome), the

terrible two's, oppositionalism, colic, excessive crying and fussing, depression, toilet training and sibling rivalry in children

5. A high demand for childhood medicines to control mood, like anti-depressant pills and Ritalin

6. Poor sense of self, because of the distanced connection between child and parent

7. A heightened rate of suicide and depression, something that did not exist in ancient times

How the Continuum Concept Benefits Babies and Children

The Continuum Concept is considered the ideal way of raising a baby. This is because of the many benefits that are offered, including:

- Better behaved children, because they are always with their mother

- Babies feel warm and loved, not abandoned while lying in a crib alone at night or sitting in a high chair

- Babies that learn to talk better, because tribal mothers do not use 'baby talk'

- Babies learn about responsible adult actions, when parents keep them close during normal adult experiences and conversation

Not only do tribal people use the Continuum Concept, there are groups in modern day Peru where mothers keep their children close. In Peru, women often fold their babies in blankets and carry them on their backs. Some women in Western societies have also adopted these principles, because of the benefits that are offered.

Next, we will discuss evidence that proves that the Continuum Concept works. Then, you will learn about the techniques necessary for this style of child rearing, including common practices that you should adopt and advice on raising your child.

Chapter Two: Evidence That Supports the Continuum Concept

If you are like most parents, you are reading this book in the hope that all the benefits offered when using the Continuum Concept have some scientific backing that proves them to be true. Otherwise, how will you know if this method has the potential for improving the way you raise your child? This chapter will provide evidence for the claims made in this book, from a biological, ancestral and psychological viewpoint.

The Importance of Development as a Child: Erikson's Stages of Psychosocial Development

If you have ever taken a basic psychology course, you may already be familiar with the incredible impact that childhood has on how a person develops into an adult. Psychologist Erik Erikson is credited with identifying these stages of psychosocial development, all of which have an impact on how a person thinks and behaves as an adult. His ideas stemmed from the psychological views of Sigmund Freud. Freud also believed in these stages, though his theories focused more on psychosexual development, while the work of Erikson focuses on psychosocial development.

At each of Erickson's stages, there is an internal crisis. This crisis involves one's own psychological development and meeting our own needs, but still adhering to societal standards. It is how one reacts to these crisis' that determines whether a positive or negative personality trait manifests. Below is what you need to know about each of the eight stages, including the parent actions/reactions that are necessary for children to have a positive developmental experience. Keep in mind that only the first five stages are reached during 'childhood', that is, up to age 18. The other three stages will be included, but will be discussed only briefly.

1. **Trust vs. Mistrust**- Children go through this experience from infancy to 1 ½ years of age. For success, the primary caregiver must provide consistent and stable care. Failure to do so allows fear to develop, while a positive experience will lead the child to have hope, especially during difficult times.

2. **Autonomy vs. Shame**- Between the ages of 1 ½ and 3, children experience this psychosocial crisis. This stage is characterized by a child's independence, as they start to make decisions about what to play with, eat, and wear. Children also start learning skills during this time. During this stage, parents should let their children explore their abilities by being supportive and patient, until the child asks for assistance. Then, it should be provided immediately to help prevent the child from feeling like a failure. When parents provide

this successfully, children find the virtue of will, which gives them a sense of security and confidence once thy are in the real world. If parents are too controlling or critical, or if the children are not given the chance to assert their independence, it can lead to doubt or shame about the child's abilities and a lack of self-esteem. Children may also become dependent on others.

3. **Initiative vs. Guilt**- Children undergo the initiative vs. guilt stage during the play age, which is between ages 3 and 5. Children are more independent in this stage, taking action toward things they want. In Western societies, parents often mistake this for aggression. Socialization is important during this stage, as children should be encouraged to make their own decisions and initiate play with others. Children also start to explore the world, both by pushing boundaries and asking questions. It is important for the primary caregiver to answer questions instead of acting like the child is a nuisance. Additionally, parents must find the balance with letting the child be independent and keeping the child safe. An abundance of guilt can make the child shy and less likely to interact with others, while a good balance helps teach the child purpose and self-control.

4. **Industry vs. Inferiority**- At what is known as the school age between 5 and 12, children undergo this fourth stage. Children are learning skills like reading, writing, mathematics, and more. A child's peer group is important during this time, because these people will start to have a greater impact on the child's self-esteem. It is important that children are competent both in school subjects and in their social life to win peer approval. Parents can help by being supportive and complimenting their child to build their self-esteem. If a child can gain peer approval, they feel confident and industrious as they tackle goals and obstacles. If they are not encouraged, but are restricted either by their parents, teacher, or peer group, they may feel inferior as they learn they are not skilled in all areas.

5. **Ego Identity vs. Role Confusion**- This crisis is experienced between the ages of 12 to 18, when a child is considered an adolescent. The adolescent years are critical ones, as the child becomes very independent. The crisis they face is discovering who they really are in the face of the physical, emotional, and mental changes that they will undergo during puberty. The child must decide who they are, both occupationally (in society) and sexually (their sex role). Parents should encourage their child to identify themselves and always be accepting of the role that the child wants to fit into.

However, pushing the child too much can have a negative impact by creating pressure that makes it harder to fall into a role. Children may also rebel when pressured too much. If the child's identity crisis is successful, the child falls into their true sense of identity, which will make them more comfortable and confident about who they are. A failed attempt in this crisis leads to role confusion, which can result in the child being unsure of themselves and lacking confidence.

6. **Intimacy vs. Isolation-** This psychosocial trait is created between the ages of 18 to 40, as a young adult. During this stage, personal relationships are extended beyond family or close friendship. Success results in feelings of commitment, security, and happiness in relationships, which teaches the virtue of unconditional love. Failure during this stage can cause emotional turmoil, as well as feelings of depression and loneliness.

7. **Generativity vs. Stagnation-** This happens during adulthood, between the years of 40-65. People commonly start to settle into societal roles, by securing their careers, choosing a life partner, and bringing up families. By raising children well and doing well at work, people develop the virtue of caring by giving back

to the community. If this stage is unsuccessful, it often results in feelings of unproductivity.

8. **Ego Integrity vs. Despair**- Even as an elderly person, the mind is still being shaped. This crisis occurs at the peak of maturity, after age 65. During this crisis, the age of retirement means that most senior citizens have a lot of spare time on their hands. Productivity slows and there is time for reflection on life. If one is satisfied with their accomplishments, they learn the virtue of wisdom to see life with a sense of completeness and accept impending death without fear. Dissatisfaction after reflection often leads to depression and a sense of hopelessness.

The ages that Erickson discussed in his theory may be slightly off for human development, especially today when children are born to younger mothers and adults may start finding love, having children and settling into a career sooner than he predicts. When Erickson's entire theory of psychosocial development is looked at, it becomes apparent that it includes stages of development that all human beings go through. It also serves as evidence that a parent's role in their child's life has profound effects on what values a child learns and where they go in life. It would make sense, therefore, that parents and children should have a close relationship, as is practiced by those using the Continuum Concept.

16

Primate Behavior

According to the theory of evolution, human beings came to be from primates, a group that includes species like orangutans, chimpanzees, and gorillas. Humans share many similar characteristics with primates and species have even been uncovered that existed between the way that primates and humans appear now. Looking at primate parenting behaviors shows that the Continuum Concept is something that is an instinct of our ancestors, both primate and human.

After birth, baby primates cling to their mother's arm. They live on her arm for several months after their birth until the baby (not the mother) is ready to detach. The mother does not constantly turn her attention to the baby, but goes about life as she normally would. The mother still looks for food, bathes, climbs and swings trees, and continues to live her life. This has two benefits. First, the baby primate learns that life is going to go on around him/her and that he/she is not the center of the universe. Second, the young primate starts to learn some of what typical life is and what will be expected of him/her.

The Yequana Tribe and Their Children's Behavior

When Liedloff encountered the Yequana tribe, it was very apparent that the children of the tribe were unlike any other children she had ever seen. Outside of the house, the children were loud, running around, swimming and whooping shouts of joy. The moment they came inside, however, the children immediately lowered their voices. They played quietly amongst themselves or served drinks and food to guests. The children did not interrupt any adult conversations and they were incredibly well behaved.

The major difference that Liedloff noted is that despite how well behaved they were, the children were incredibly happy. They had not been oppressed or disciplined to reach this state. It was just natural to them. This sparked Liedloff's curiosity and she would return several times to study the Yequana tribe. The major difference that she saw was the way children were raised. Even when the child was an infant, the members of the tribe practiced different child rearing tactics than those used in Western cultures.

Something that is incredibly important to remember is that the Continuum Concept is not about putting your life on hold to coddle your child. They can be in your arms as an infant and explore when they are ready, but you should still go about life as you would normally without a child. This is critical to ensure that the parenting technique you are using is not child-centered. Finding balance is important, because the Continuum Concept does not work for kids who believe they are the center of the universe. You can still respond to a child's needs immediately (or within a proper timeframe), but you must not make them feel as if they are the most important being in the world. Otherwise, you may find that despite how kind, caring, and self-giving that you are, by the time your child is a toddler they be having temper tantrums when they do not get exactly what they want.

Chapter Three: Basic Guidelines for Child Rearing Using the Continuum Concept

Now that you understand what the Continuum Concept is, it is time to learn about what the guidelines for the continuum concept are. As you read, keep in mind that there is a perfect balance for many of these techniques. It is very possible to be too placating, just as it is possible to be neglectful. Without further ado, it is time to discuss the child rearing techniques of the Continuum Concept.

#1: Constant Contact

Under the Continuum Concept, parents are encouraged to have close contact with their children from the day of their birth. This means that after the child has exited the mother, it should be immediately placed with the parents. The parents should clean it and if measurements are needed, the parents should accompany it. Many Western cultures take the child to check the baby's health after birth and males are often subjected to traumatic circumcisions. This can create incredible mental harm, even though the baby is only minutes old.

The child, instead of being placed in a bassinet or playpen, should stay in the parents' arms as they go about their daily tasks. While the child should have a primary caretaker who is with the child most of the time, the child can also share close contact with either parent or other care takers.

Parents should continue to hold the child regularly until the child is ready to let go. The child will observe what the parent is doing, be it washing dishes, preparing dinner, or reading a book. By observing, the child is learning. They are also learning that even though they are close to their parents, they are not always the center of their parent's focus. This observation, while sleeping and awake, is called passive participation. In addition to learning and observing, the child is able to discharge the energy they have accumulated through the parent's movements and activities. Discharging this energy is important. Unlike children raised using Western standards, babies on the Continuum Concept are not trapped in a crib. This allows them to use their energy stores without having to kick or scream to get attention. This energy discharge also allows babies to fall asleep easily. The babies do not need rocked, because they have sufficiently used their energy stores.

#2: Co-Sleeping

Co-sleeping is another important principle, because it is recommended that parents keep their infant close even when sleeping. Parents should continue to co-sleep with their child until children are ready to wean themselves and move into their own beds. Usually, children co-sleep with their parents for the first two years before they are mature enough to make the decision to sleep alone. This prevents the child from feeling lonely and isolated, as is common when children are put to bed alone or encouraged to 'cry it out' and cry themselves to sleep. Children who are put to bed using the 'cry it out' method may also feel abandoned by their parents, or ashamed of themselves.

#3: Separating When the Baby is Ready

Even children raised using the Continuum Concept do not stay in their parents' arms forever. There will come a time when your baby is ready to leave your arms, and that should be encouraged. Allow your baby to break from your hold and into full freedom as soon as they are ready. Let them learn to crawl and explore the world around them. However, be sure to pick them up when they are ready. Always receive the child immediately if they are ready to come back to your arms, especially in the earlier days of this stage. This will give the child a sense of security so that they continue to explore.

As your child matures, you will notice they will spend more time out of your arms. Do not feel saddened by this, but allow the child to learn and explore on their own. Proper response during this stage of your infant's life is necessary for the baby to learn autonomy. Eventually, this autonomy will show as the child preferring to roam over being in their parent's arms. They will typically only return during a stressful situation, when they require feelings of safety and comfort.

#4: Appropriately Responding to the Child's Needs

Finding the balance between indulgence and deprivation is critical for this technique. As a parent, you should be there when your child needs you. Instead of pushing a feeding schedule on your child, you should allow them to feed naturally. Wait for your infant's cue and then breastfeed as it is requested. As you breastfeed, though, it is important that you continue with your adult activities. You should also respond to toileting and other basic needs as your baby expresses his/her discomfort. However, you must do this in a way that the child is not the center of attention.

#5: Trust Your Child's Survival Mechanisms

One of the mistakes that new parents often make as their infant starts exploring on their own is being over-protective. When you do not let a child explore and get hurt, they do not have a chance to earn to be self-protective. They will not take cautions and may get into trouble, because they expect that their parents will always save them. It is important to let your baby roam as they please, provided the area is safe from anything that can seriously harm the child. Let them crawl in and out of a laundry basket or look through magazines on the coffee table. Trust in your baby and your child will eventually learn to trust in themselves.

#6: Respond Appropriately to Crying

It is not uncommon for parents using Western child rearing techniques to use the 'cry it out' method. This is either used because the parent is busy and neglects to tend to the crying or because the parent holds the belief that responding to crying immediately will spoil the child. However, neither of the ideas are true.

Imagine how terrifying the 'cry it out' method can be for a child. Imagine how a child feels if their parent is out of the room and they are trapped in a playpen or crib. They would feel incredibly lonely and unsure, not knowing if their parents are listening to their cries or when they are going to respond. It is equally as traumatizing if the parent is in the room and not responding, if not more. The child can see their parent and is crying out to them, but their needs are being ignored. This can cause the child to feel neglected, alone, and even insignificant in the eyes of their parent.

When children are raised using the Continuum Concept, they do not cry out for attention. They cry because something is wrong, whether they are uncomfortable, hungry, or do not feel safe. The parent should immediately respond to this crying, giving it validation. When responding, it is important not to be displeased, judgmental, or invalidating of the child's needs. However, it is equally as important not to show excess concern or create the idea that the child is the center of the parent's attention.

#7: Set Expectations for Social Cooperativeness

It is important that babies learn what is expected from them by their parents. Children should always feel welcomed in the presence of company, though they should not be allowed to interrupt adults. They should feel worthy of being in the presence of their parents and others, because they should sense their parents' expectations. Upon being raised using the Continuum Concept, in addition to sensing their role, the child will fulfill that role.

Chapter Four: Shaping Your Child: Guide, Don't Punish

The reason that children raised using the Continuum Concept are so well-behaved is because parents use different tactics than those in Western culture. Continuum Concept children are not scolded, put in timeout and left to cry, spanked, or otherwise punished. Instead, the children learn what is expected of them and they fulfill this role. Parents do this with proper guidance and by setting the example for what they expect from their child.

Why Children Act Out

Unlike some parents believe, children do not act out because they are 'spoiled' because their parents are attentive. Rather, children act out because parents sometimes become over-permissive. Children misbehave when they are unsure of their parent's actions. When children are raised using the Continuum Concept since birth, they learn to become observers. They watch their parents' behaviors as a way to know what will be expected from them.

When a parent stops in the middle of tasks to turn their attention to a baby who is not crying and who is content at the time, they create a feeling of uncertainty. It shortens the expectations for the child, because they see their parent stopping what they are doing to turn their attention to them. In turn, children begin to question the parent's ability, because it becomes apparent that he or she cannot focus on their own expectations. Additionally, when a parent constantly turns their focus to their child, they begin to take signals from the child. This is not seen as a bonding experience, but as a lack of confidence. The parent appears to be looking to the child for guidance, which is when the child starts to think that their parent is not a role model but someone they must give guidance to.

How to Prevent Bad Behavior in Children

It is how a parent conducts themselves and how they interact with their child that has such a profound effect on a child's behavior in the future. At all times, the parent must remain sure of him or herself and project feelings of calmness and competency. When the child regularly receives these feelings from the parent, they will not question their authority. This is the reason that babies raised using the Continuum Concept are so willing to sense and then fulfill parent expectations.

When children sense feelings of uncertainty in their parents, they will naturally try to push the parent's limits. They are looking for the time where their parent will remain firm, calm, and sure of themselves and this is what they set as the limit. Now, imagine that a mother is trying desperately to please her child. The child does something like coloring a picture on the wall and the mother then asks, in an apologetic voice, that the child does not do it again. Instead of complying, the child is going to sense this apologetic tone and continue to do the behavior. Then, when the mother takes the child's coloring utensils to prevent the incident, the child will become enraged. In response, the mother pleads with the child to behave or may try to explain. As the child senses the mother's desperate tone, he/she will make even more unacceptable demands. This will continue until the parent regains their composure, removing authority from the child and resuming their calm, sure place in existence.

Parents using the Continuum Concept must know that when the child tries to control how their parent behaves, it is because the child wants to be sure of the adult in charge. He/she does not necessarily want to succeed in disarming their parent of power, but rather, wants to succeed in knowing that the person in charge actually knows what they are doing.

The other side of being a parent in charge is setting the example. How can you swear in front of a child or lash out in anger at your partner and not expect the child to do the same? You set the expectations for your child by showing them, not telling them. They look to their parent constantly for guidance, from the moment they are brought into this world. Children exit the womb as a blank canvas, ready to learn and behave exactly as they are taught. This means that the parental role in a child's life is critical, from the moment of birth, to the child growing into a healthy, well-rounded, and productive being. This existence is one that leads to great children, who will grow into the adults of the future and contribute to society on a community or even a global level.

Conclusion

Thank you again for downloading this book! Now that you have reached the end of it, you should have an understanding of the Continuum Concept in its totality. This way of child rearing is natural and has been around since the beginning of mankind. Even primates have practiced a non-child focused upbringing that maximizes the amount of contact children have with their parents.

By choosing to raise your children using the Continuum Concept, you are ensuring that they will be well-behaved, but still happy in their existence. This parenting concept allows kids to be kids, but still teaches them to be contributing and respectful.

Do not worry if you already have children and have not yet raised them using the Continuum Concept. It is never too late to change your parenting tactics to raise a happy, healthy and well-rounded child.

Best of luck as you continue on your parenting journey!

Made in the USA
Coppell, TX
18 September 2020